Res Burman's
Poet

Volume

RES J. F. BURMAN

Writers' Champion

The right of Res J. F Burman to be identified as the author of this work has been asserted in accordance with sections 77 and 78 of the Copyright Design and Patent Act 1988.

Copyright © Res J. F. Burman 2022
For information contact via email: res.burman@outlook.com

All text materials taken from John's on line blog: http://resswritingandpoetry.blogspot.co.uk

Published through Writers'Champion imprint of MAPublisher (Penzance)
www.mapublisher.org.uk, email: mapublisher@yahoo.com

Printed in UK through Print on demand

ISBN-13: 978-1-910499-92-4

Book layout, typesetting and cover designed by Mayar Akash
Cover image by Cam de Pete
Typeset in Times Roman

Paper printed on is FSC Certified, lead free, acid free, buffered paper made from wood-based pulp. Our paper meets the ISO 9706 standard for permanent paper. As such, paper will last several hundred years when stored.

Content

Introduction

You're holding in your hands a collection of the poems of Res J.F. Burman, an old soldier, a world traveller, a Taoist, a father, a photographer, a woodturner, and a man known by many as the Pirate of Penzance. Res is a man who is beloved by many readers in far-flung places, one who has outlived his contemporaries and now faces the loneliness of life's later years with courage and grace.

Res writes of what he knows. Whether commenting on his war experiences, his luck and blessings in love, his encounters with Leonard Cohen in London, his time in Matala in Greece where a young Joni Mitchell found inspiration leading to Carey and to her masterful Blue album, Res reveals the gentle mastery of a man who has seen a lot and written of it humbly, with heart and wisdom. And when he speaks of his pain and fury, addressing challenges and injustices, Res does so with authority.

Where Res lives in Penzance he has a unique and steadfast view of the world, of the sea and the changing skies. He celebrates the glories and mercies of his days through writing and photography, sharing them across the globe with people who've come to know and love his work. This book is a testament to his goodness and talents, a book that marks a victory of the human kind, a survival of storms, a man's ongoing search for meaning, for what truly matters in life.

Doug Lang
Vancouver, Canada Musician, Prairie Poet and Radio DJ at "Better Days" and "Riverside Drive" on Vancouver Co-op Radio.

Res Burman is what I call a "Vast" person. He is a person who in his personality, his interests, his experiences, his perceptions, and his talents takes in much of this world in which we live. He has a deep understanding of the human condition combined with the ability to express his understanding with a clear, compassionate, poetic language to which we all can relate.

Res has worked in various professions which include two that might seem poles apart. He was a soldier overseas for a number of years in Her Majesty's service. His interest in and curiosity about the places where he served combined with his natural compassion led him to not only take great interest in the cultures but also to get to know, understand, and care for the people. These experiences made Res a man of the Eastern World as well as a man of the Western World. This gives his poetry its distinctive flavor.

Res has also worked in the profession of animal husbandry. He has a wide ranging knowledge, understanding, and love of animals, both domesticated and wild. The subject of his poetry often deals with mankind's relationship with animals and our inner-dependence with them. His poetic images often express the human need for a relationship with the animal kingdom and all of nature, emphasizing the importance of an appreciation of the beauty and power of the natural world which so often has a spiritual nature.

Res has lived a life that has combined both the spiritual as well as the practical. Working as a carpenter he has been able to bring together his craftsmanship with his artistic perceptions as a cabinet maker.

The ruggedly beautiful ocean shoreline of Cornwall and the Penzance area have provided a backdrop that has inspired his poetic musings for many years and, more recently, another of his artistic hobbies, photography.

His poems range in motif from the especially serious subject of the spiritual world all the way to a satirical sense of humor expressing thoughts about the absurdities of life. As I think of Robert Frost to be the "American Poet" whose poetry touches on ideas to which all humans can relate, so I think of Res as being the "English Poet" whose poems are wide ranging and express ideas to which all humans can relate. Res is truly the gentlemanly, pirate, Poet of Penzance.

James Wesley Farmer
Singer/songwriter, poet and writer of prose, teacher, and 1st Mate to Cap'n Res Burman

Res Burman's poetry is like a cool wind, the softest ocean in the summer & a bright blue sky filled with the echo of singing birds. His words surround you like a playful & passionate lover who swims inside your heart and mind.

His biggest fan,
Gina Nemo
Gina Nemo is an American actress, singer, author, poet and marketing executive who had an award-winning role as Dorothy Pezzino in the American television series 21 Jump Street in the 1980s. She runs her own Film Actors School. She is the daughter of jazz musician Henry Nemo.

Res is a national treasure and this spills forth in his poetry telling of life, love, bygone times and of his many adventures.

His strong compassion for his fellow man shines throughout and it is obvious that Res is a man with much heart. I'm sure yours will be touched many times while reading his poems.

He has a knack for that and also for bringing alive stories of old with emotions and images vividly painted in all their diversity. I feel blessed to know Res and privileged to have gained a glimpse into his extraordinary life told through his poetry.

I'm sure you will too.

Tina Purplenblue Clowes Kay.
Hill Walker, Poet and Photographer Extraordinaire.

A Postcard from Kuching

A postcard arrived here today
From a land that James Brooke cried for
That took me back to the rifles crack,
And the land I almost died for!
To the rivers and seas, the jungle trees,
And the island of Borneo,
And a dirty little war and so much more
Fifty long years ago!

I was twenty-one and just one day,
'Twas time I earned my shilling!*
A silver 'plane carried me away
Judged old enough for killing!
Little I knew, as away we flew
They'd sent me to Sarawak.
And over the years, through smiles and tears
That land still calls me back!

James Brooke had been the Rajah there,
His rule was fair but stern.
You could feel his hand upon that land
At almost every turn.
The people had loved him dearly
And his rule had stood the test
And now many years later
The land was different to the rest!

Bung 'Karno* sent his troops raiding
Far and wide across the border.
Attacking defenceless people
So we went to bring back order!
We went because we had to,
But what was unexpected,
Was how much we came to love,
Those dear people we protected.

Jungle longhouse, kampong, town,
Back at Police HQ
From the people of that blessed land
Kindness was all we knew!
Though force of arms protected

The friendly people on our side
In the end what really mattered,
'Twas "Hearts and Minds" that turned the tide.

Now as this postcard reaches me,
Time and distance calls me back,
Is it to sweat and blood, the bloody mud,
Or the whip-lash rifles crack?
No, it's laughing eyes so deep you'd drown,
And voices that would say
"We love you, love you, love you here,
Oh won't you, won't you stay?"

We were always welcomed back,
People hugged us and they kissed us
From jungle swamp or mountain track.
They told us they had missed us,
Long-house base or back in town
Gave us fruit and sat us down.

Then we'd eat and drink so hearty
Every meeting was a party!
Be it song or poem to entertain
Christian Hindu Taoist Jain
Everyone would do their party pieces!
For there we had brothers uncles nieces!

Never a thought of racial strife
Would mar these peaceful peoples life.
Whether we slept 'neath trophy heads,
Or cool on silk on Chinese Beds,
We'd friends in the market, thick as thieves,
We ate fried rice off banana leaves.

I remember well the wind in palms,
The friendly market places,
The clasp of silky dusky arms,
The beauty in their faces.
I remember all the kindnesses,
The words and touch of love,
And oh! Those magic tropic skies,
And the dawns that bloomed above.

Only a simple postcard, fifty cents or so
And satu ringgit* postage to days so long ago
And there it sat on my mat as if 'twas yesterday,
When kit and gun, and me so young, once again away!
But that is just a fancy of an old man's mind,
But how I yearn once more to turn to those people kind.

I still sometimes smell the markets there,
But no MeeHoon Soup for many a year.
But it's little things that call my heart a-while,
The loving words that taught me how to smile.

Even today, people say, Sarawak is different, through and through,
And those of us whom Sarawak touched, we are all different too!

*Earned my shilling = Taking the Kings (or Queens) Shilling = Joining
the Army or Navy and possibly Air Force, (though they'd have wanted
more than a shilling!)
*Bung 'Karno - Brother 'Karno - President Soekarno of Indonesia.
*Satu ringgit - One Malaysian Dollar.

16th October 2012

My Woods

Buzzard flies over
The woodland that I planted
Oh to see his view

29th October 2012

Lola

Sweet little Lola
Mardi Gras Queen of the West
Her Mother's darling

23rd October 2012

Such Eyes

She had such eyes
You could drown in... and here's me
Just learning to swim

22nd October 2012

Blue Eyes

She had oceans
In her blue eyes... and left me
With salt tears in mine

21st October 2012

Here Be Dragons

In the morning sky
I thought I saw a dragon
Heaven's messenger

20th October 2012

Inspired by Gabi San of
https://www.facebook.com/groups/poetryjoysofjapan/

Angry Sea

The wind brings the sea
Angry now into the Bay
Autumn storms dying

17th October 2012

International Day for the Eradication of Poverty

International
Day for the Eradication
Of Poverty... Aum

17th Octo0ber 2012

Hungry Jackdaw Haiku(ish)

The bamboo is battered
And the jackdaw is hungry
Cool autumn sunshine

16th October 2012

Decorations

A telephone call
Do I want my medals engraved?
49 years late

They were not so keen
To hand out decorations
When the sh*t hit the fan

Just in time to go
On the lid of my coffin
My grateful country

At least HM the Queen
Sends me my pocket money
Regularly…

Bless Her

17th October 2012

My Beauty Of The Low Lands

She was small and beautiful
A youthful bloom seemed to shine
From beneath her sun tanned skin
Her blonde hair like corn silk
Framing her exquisite face
And she was my companion
For the bumpy bus ride
From Matala on the south coast of Crete
Over the mountains to Iráklion

We had talked a time or two
In the taverna society of Matala.
Danced a time or two at the Mermaid Café
Not knowing how famous it would become
From Joni Mitchell's 'Carey'.
But she was too beautiful
For a tired old soldier like me to pursue
And she was always surrounded
By those wanting to share her beauty
Or her body! While the wind
Carried the smell of African dust
As we danced in the night.

When she talked to you
She had a habit of stepping closer
Right into one's personal space
And looking directly up into your eyes
With those eyes so deep blue
They were almost violet.
And although she was surrounded
By admirers,
For those brief moments of conversation
It was as though we were quite alone in the world.
She had a calm, often serious, beauty
But when she smiled at you
The smile not only lit up her lovely face
It seemed to light up one's life as well.

Now tired from the farewell parties
We shared a seat on the bus.
Her bare arm touching mine

As we talked about our mutual friends
And acquaintances among the freaks
And draft dodgers, deserters and ex-soldiers
That made up the floating population
Of Matala in those days.
She told me her name was Helena
Which, she said, meant light,
A perfect name for this shining beauty.
Gradually she grew sleepy
Her head nodding until it rested
Upon my delighted shoulder.

I hardly moved for the rest of the journey
For fear of waking her.
I could smell the clean perfume of her hair
Feel the softness of her skin
Where her cheek rested on my arm.
See the beguiling white Vee
Where her suntan faded
Between her perfect breasts.
My breathing slowed as almost
In a state of meditation I sat there
Loving the trust and closeness,
The warmth and the beauty
Of Lovely Helena from the Low Countries.
And while the Greeks around us
Fervently crossed themselves
At every roadside cross and shrine
Commemorating every fatal accident
On that twisty mountain road
I sat there wishing the journey
Would go on forever.

Eventually we rattled down
From the mountains into Iráklion.
I bought a ticket on the Ferry
With the money I had received
From 'selling' my cave on
To its next occupant.
That was the way on leaving Matala.
You always 'sold' your cave for the price
Of the bus fare over the mountains
And the Ferry ride back to the mainland.

We shared the Ferry ride
Helena and I, across the Aegean Sea to Piraeus
Athens' seaport, busy bustling and earthy.
We took a room together in a cheap hotel.
It was only when I went to the bathroom
And spied girls standing in the dim doorways
Of their rooms that I realised that
We had taken a room in what served
Piraeus as a Brothel! Complete with
Government Rules and Regulations
Printed behind the doors.
I made sure that I accompanied my
Beautiful friend to and from the bathroom
After that! But we both found it funny,
And perhaps it added a little to our passion,
But none to the tenderness that grew
Between us that night.

Tenderness like a balm to my old wounds.
It was there I learned she had deliberately
Chosen to travel alone with me,
Away from the competition of her attendants!
She could switch from Dutch to German,
To English to French, easier than I could
Change hats! But she said, "French is the
Language of Love, monchéri"
"Rather than the gutteral language of my own country!"

She said she had always collected
Injured birds and animals,
That was why she wanted to become a
Veterinary Surgeon.
I asked her, "Is that what I am to you
An injured bird?"
"Mais non, monchéri, but I have always
Had a way with injuries! To me you are
An injured horse, non? Like the knights
Used to ride!" She didn't know that
My Chinese Horoscope sign
Was the Horse.
"Now you must learn to let
Your scars dance, just as we did

At the Mermaid Café!" And we danced
Naked, to a tinny radio in a Brothel
In salty earthy Piraeus.

Next day we took the lovely wooden tram
Up the line to Athens.
There to go our separate ways.
She to join friends for the overland journey
Across Albania and Yugosolavia to Austria.
I, forbidden that route by my Government,
Unwilling to allow the secrets I still carried
In my head, to venture behind the Iron Curtain,
Was forced to remain in Athens.
Sleeping on a camp bed on the roof of a Hotel
In the centre of the city.
Waiting for a cheap passage on a *Gastarbeiter bum boat
Carrying poor Greeks across the Ionian Sea
To Brindisi in Italy and thence overland
To a life of servitude in Germany.

We exchanged names and addresses
She writing hers on the flyleaf
Of my copy of The Lord of the Rings
Still only part read despite six months in the Islands.
And so we parted! She, again surrounded
By admirers, but stepping away once more
Into my personal space for one last kiss,
As her attendants glowered behind her back!

It was a couple of months before I heard
Leonard Cohen sing 'Sisters of Mercy'
On an LP in a bed-sit in Notting Hill.
And a year or two before I met the man himself.
But 'Sisters of Mercy' became
Always our song in my mind!
Lord of the Rings was washed to a pulp
As I hitch-hiked through the Alps
Her name and address dissolving into
Wet sludge in the bottom of a rucksack pocket.

I did eventually buy another copy
But the name and address of lovely Helena
Was sadly absent from the flyleaf!

I did eventually finish Tolkien's saga
But every mention of Hobbit Holes
Cast my mind back to when I too
Lived in a Hobbit Hole on a Cretan cliff face
In the ancient land of the Minotaur.
And on leaving spent two loving days
With the most beautiful girl in the world!

If I had known then what I know now………(Sigh)

15th October 2012

* Gastarbeiter = Guest Worker, in Germany. In those days many poor
Greeks took ship to Italy and then overland to Germany to make money
as Labourers in Germany's expanding economy. As a consequence of
that, I learned more German in six months in Greece than I did in two
years in Germany. The Germans spoke too good English to allow us to
mutilate their language by holding conversations with us in German!

Window Guardians

Window Guardians
Watch and wait so patiently
Lucky Cat beckons

8th October 2012

St Michael's Mount

Autumn clouds rise slow
Reluctant to leave the arms
Of St Michael's Mount

8th October 2012

Gold Earring

Advisory
This poem contains swearing
If you are likely to be offended
Don't read it!

I have long been enamoured
Of the Greek Sailor's belief
Of wearing a Gold Earring
In order to pay the ferryman
For the journey across the Styx
It seems to indicate a preparedness
To face one's death
As willingly as one's life.

Cut to Market Jew Street
In Penzance.
The Cornish swear it has
Nothing to do with Jews
But me and the Rabbi
Have our doubts!

I always walk up and down
That street
About three inches off the railings
So no one will expect
An Old Gimpy like me
To leap out of their way!

One day a Wee Blister of a man
Charged the three inch gap
Kicking my walking stick
Out from under me
And almost knocking me over!

He stopped and glared
About twelve paces beyond me.
"You haven't got any f***ing right
To be on this f***ing pavement
Waving that f***ing walking stick about
Like a f***ingnancy boy!"
He shouted at me!

I whispered a little Taoist prayer
For all the sexes
Girls, boys and hairdressers!
"I'll show him!" I thought
And went straight down to Wharfside
And got myself
A Greek Sailors Gold Earring!
I was very careful which ear
They put it in!

Just wait till I see Wee Blister again
I thought.
"Oi! F***wit!" I'll cry.
"Look at my f****ing earring!
That's on the heterosexual side!"

But I probably won't!
When you find some arse
Down in a hole
Covered in sh*t,
What's the point
Of jumping in there with him?

But at least I'm ready
To face the ferryman
And anything else
That life or death
Or any Wee Blister
May throw in my direction!

14th October 2012

This is a true story.

Duke Lang's Better Days.

Vancouver Co-op Radio

A collection of Haiku(ish) Verses
about or inspired by
Duke Lang's Better Days Radio Show

Today's dawn chorus
Was Vancouver Radio
Duke Lang's late night show

Listen in the West
Post some Haiku in the South
The East still beckons

Duke Lang's Better Days
Waking the Penzance seagulls
For their morning piracy

I hear from Vancouver
Of Tokyo quakes... small world
In peril

Iris Dement
If you'd sing... I'd listen
Till the cows came home

Larry John Wilson
Gone now but not forgotten
Leaving us his songs

A fine singer pass'd
With his laugh and his singing
Ringing in our ears

Listening in the night
Tuning into Vancouver
Better days

12th October 2012

Ode to Eve Elliott

Old Causewayhead just ain't the same
I don't know who is to blame
But the street has turned to a dreary mile
Without the sunshine of your smile

Nowhere to stop for a welcome kiss
I admit it's that I truly miss
No smile lighting up my day
Now that you have gone away

No wonder Penzance is in decline
All year round it's winter time
Ashes to ashes dust to dust
Perhaps I'll move out to St Just

Perhaps by bus or perhaps by car
I'll never more eat a Grizzly Bar

9th October 2012

Autumn Mist

Autumn mist
The Mount hides coyly
Above the clouds

8th October 2012

Old Charlie

My old sarong's faded
But my Viet Cong pyjamas
Are still going strong

Old Charlie ~ he always was
Damn near indestructible

30th September 2012

Gandhara Buddha

Gandhara Buddha
On a lucky red necklace
His hand on my heart

Gandhara Buddha
His hand resting on my chest
His smile in my heart

Gandhara Buddha
Hanging around my neck
His wisdom in my heart

Hopefully!

30th September 2012

Thanks to Dr Gabi Greve San for the inspiration

Bugis Street

Old Bugis Street was quite a sight
With acetylene lamps burning bright
Tables and chairs from end to end
Where you could meet and greet a friend

And order food from any stall
Those cooks all at your beck and call
Sharks Fin Soup, Thousand Year Eggs
And strange things done to chicken legs

Nasi Goreng, satay, saffron rice
Octopus and Tiger Prawns so nice
Tiger beer and Anchor too
San Miguel, now there's a brew
So when all the bars of Singapore
Switched off their lights and locked the door
You could still eat and drink all night
And Bugis Street set my heart alight

There were Lady-boys and Chinese Whores

And sailors in from foreign shores
Bush pilots resting from their flights
And soldiers resting from their fights

Rubber tappers from Malaya way
Tin miners down in town to stay
And spotless children playing tic-tac-toe
And winning - watch your money go

There'd be smugglers resting from the sea
And traders in from far Araby
Ginseng dealers trading fair
You'd find all sorts of commerce there

Gun runners just in from the isles
Soldiers from the rank and files
Young ladies from the Embassies
Doing just about what they please

Pirates, pimps and taxi drivers
Royal Marines and pearl divers
All the flotsam of a great sea port
Gathered there to take their sport

Family and friends would come and meet
Right there in what was Bugis Street
Bulldozed now - and it don't seem right
For Bugis Street was my delight

29th September 2012

Singapore Annie

Singapore Annie
Was eighty if a day
And a hard life
Had written it's story
Upon her raddled face

She'd graciously sit
And accept a drink

From guys on Bugis Street
Among the beautiful
Lady-boys

And the smart
Spotless kids
Who'd clean one's shoes
Or play tic-tac-toe
For money
And always
Eventually win!

Annie earned her way
By hailing Mercedes taxis.
She wanted her special friends
To ride home in style.
And the drivers and her friends
Paid her a commission

When she knew you well
She'd coyly slide the hem
Of her cheongsam
Up her aged leg
And show a tattoo
A Highland Soldier
Painted upon her thigh.

Then from her handbag
She'd carefully take
A letter, much mended
With sticky stamp borders
It was dated long before
World War Two.

Then she'd ask one
To read the letter to her.
She'd sit with the glitter
Of tears
In her ancient eyes
As one read the words
Of a Soldier
Long dead.

Who had
Been enamoured
Of her beauty
And obviously
Loved her dearly

Who says that
An Old Whore
Has no heart?

28th September 2012

Young Eyes

Goddess grant nothing
Will sully that look of trust
In her sweet young eyes

27th September 2012

Cool Breeze

Cool breeze
Brings autumn to my room
The Goddess smiles

27th September 2012

My Honoured House Guests

People run through rain
The dogs and I warm and dry
My honoured house guests

26th September 2012

Cool Breath On My Skin

Cool breath on my skin
Autumn steals into my room
The curtains tremble

26th September 2012

The Pale Hands of the Goddess

The lily opens
The pale Hands of the Goddess
Holding a Golden Heart

25th September 2012

Elephant

Elephant all dressed up
For a festival... Dreaming
Of the next sugar cane

24th September 2012

Médecins Sans Frontières

Taking care to where
It is needed most... Angels
Médecins Sans Frontières

24th September 2012

Dogs

There are times when dogs
Are ready for anything
And times when they're NOT

24th September 2012

Who Am I?

I have noticed
Over the years
Whatever you wake up with
Whatever state of health
Or mind
Whatever advantages
You may have
Whatever shortcomings
These are the tools
Unequal though they be
With which you
Must face the day.

Whatever day you wake up to
Fine or foul
Hot or cold
Peace or war
Pain or gain
Challenge
Or tribulation
Captivity or
Freedom
This is YOUR day

It's how you handle it
That determines
Who you are
Not whether you
Win or lose
But if you tried
If you did the
Decent thing
If you helped
Instead of hindered
If you praised
Rather than cursed
If you loved
Rather than hated
Did your best
And not your worst!

If you have seen
Every member
Of your species
As Sister or Brother
And Race or religion
Or colour as just
The icing on the cake
Little variations
That make Brother
And Sister
Interesting
To each other
Not different

Who am I?
I'm just one of the crowd
Who am I?
I'm just one of US!

16th March 2008

Kuan Yin and Lao Tzu

Give me wise men's words
And the Goddess of Mercy
What more could I need

Pulled by Kuan Yin's gentle hand
The voice of Lao Tzu calling

24th September 2012

Water Aid

I have clean water
I give that others may drink
Free from fear

23rd September 2012

Lao Tzu

Confucius he say
"Given a few more years
Of life to finish my study
Of the Book of Changes
And I may be free from great errors!"

Just goes to show
What a Big-head
Confucious was!

Lao Tzu smiled
And whispered
"The beginning of all things
Lies still in the beyond,
In the form of ideas
Yet to become real"

We both smiled
And walked on
Arm in arm.
Playing Ping-pong
With ideas of Love

Xiao Gao Jiao, Little Longhorn,
Munched contentedly
On fresh grass and water chestnuts
I'd gathered for him
Kind brown eyes liquid
With loving wisdom
Too slow and deep
For me to understand.

"When will you get to the West
Master?" I asked.
"When can I expect to see you
Riding down Causwayhead in Penzance,
On your water buffalo?"

The Old Man smiled
Put a finger to his lips,
"Ah you Westerners," he said fondly,

"Better to live in wonder
Than just wondering!"

With a twinkle in his eye,
He squeezed my arm and said,
"Little Brother, if you thought less
And felt more, you'd know
I'm already there with you!"

The passage made by Confucious is from his Analects
The passage made by Lao Tzu is from the Book Of Changes. The I
Ching

29th February 2008

Swelling

When you can HEAR
Your feet SWELLING
Over the hum of the computer

You know you've been
Writing too many
Haiku

Time to put
One's feet
Up

Don't laugh
I'm not a
Footballer

We Old
South China Seas
Hands

Are entitled to
Wear a sarong
When the feeling takes us

These were my feet

When I was
A younger man

Before oedema
And medications
Raised their ugly heads!

24th September 2012

And these are the feet
Of an older man.
Still wearing the sarong though!

My Old Lathe

Up in the attic
My old lathe now sits dreaming
Of REVOLUTIONS!

Rocking Horse droppings
Collect on the attic floor
Woodworm's detritus

3rd September 2012

Door

Staining my front door
After 10 years non-smoking
Brown stained fingers again

23rd September 2012

Star Crossed Lovers

Star crossed lovers
A broken willow plate
Even the bamboos weep

23rd September 2012

Listening to Leonard Tanka

Listening to Leonard
Five discs running back to back
Happy Birthday ~ Friend

I'm richer for knowing you
I've shared you joys and sorrows

You bought honey
And tears and shared them with us
And we have loved you

And certainly will always be
Poet Laureate to us all

Hallelujah

22nd September 2012

Dining With The God Of War

KuanYü and I
Two old soldiers share a meal
Peace rains down on us

22nd September 2012

Bovine Love

She rubs against me
Like an affectionate cat
Half a ton of love

22nd September 2012

Pluto Bear and Drackle

Old dog dreams of youth
Resting there in the sunshine
Old goose stands his watch

22nd September 2012

Dogwood

Do dogs know it's dogwood?
Or are they alakefic
Will any old stick do?

22nd September 2012

Eastern Promise

Hint of Sandalwood
My mind flies back to the East
Your soft sweet kisses

22nd September 2012

Ray and Ollie

Ray and Ollie
Flying mane and feathers
And a two wheeled cart

21st September 2012

Weather Report

There be squalls
Here in Penzance
Chasing each other
Across roof~tops
Of houses and cars

Dashing themselves
Into vapour
On all surfaces.
Death-sliding down
Roofs ~ over edges
Launders and gutters
Down~pipes overflowing

Making raging rivers
In miniature
Down the steep streets
Leading to the sea.
Causing little dams
Of rubbish to form
Behind the wheels
Of parked cars

Last night's take away
Making a dash
For freedom
To evade
The hungry gulls
School girls squeal
As each cold gust
Hits them
Too fashion conscious
To wear a coat
Or carry a 'brolly

Visibility closes down
As each squall hits
Opens again as sight
Follows the squall
Into the distance

And between each squall
Sunny spells shining
On the washed clean
Streets

The street cleaners
Will be happy
All the rubbish
Is at the bottom
Of the hill!

18th January 2008

Waveform Poems

Above the wave crest
A shaft of winter sunshine
Lights it's path to shore
Between reef markers
Ravenous breakers rush in
Hungry for the shore
Stapled granite walls
Help protect the railway line
From the hungry sea

3rd December 2009

Tulip Petal Love

Tulip petals on a book of poetry
Upon the bed where they fell
Would they hint at morning whispers
Morning dreams, if they could tell?

1st December 2007

To Samarkand

Written in answer to "The Librarian Requests Your Attention" by
Mademoiselle Omnisciente

Ah, to Samarkand with Flecker or Cathay with old Marco,
Or round the Horn with good Zeng He, so many years ago.
And when I was a soldier out there in the mire
We fought FOR running women and to save their homes from fire.

I'm written through with sagas and tales of misspent youth
And sufferings, wars and glories and that old search for the truth
And simple soldiers poetry that tell the tales of Old
And Beasts who came into your life to save them from the cold!

But when it comes to lessons, my slate is clean and clear
And so I come to sit with you, I come to sit and hear.

18th August 2007

Francoise

There is a poise
An elegance
In your pose.
A stillness
That speaks
Of the freedom
Of the Dance

24th October 2009

The Apple To Eve

You did not tempt me
With that apple.
T'was not you
Led me astray.
I ate of it
And Oh so gladly
So that with you
I might stay!

Oh I dearly loved
The Garden
But that Paradise,
I freely state,
Would be a
Damned
Hell on earth
Without thee
My Beloved

12th Feb 2006

Shop Houses

I love shop houses
Cool shady five foot walk-ways
Treasures of the East

16th September 2012

Storms, Squalls and Tempests

Making love
While
The rain
Beats
On our window

Matching our rhythm
And our pauses
Increasing
In intensity
Building

Like handfuls
Of gravel
Flung
Urging us
On

Squalls
Whipping us
To a frenzy
Higher
And higher

The cold
On the window
Overcome
By the Heat
In you

The cold wet
Of the rain
Washed away
By your liquid
Fire

Outside
Winter storms
Here with us
Volcanic
Paradise

You are my squall
My tempest
My Goddess
Let me bathe
In your storm

Let me lie
in the sunshine
on the beach
Of your
Spent passion

Forever

21st January 2000

Ray On Cats

My friend Ray,
Living in the woods,
At Westmoor.
Making tea on
His woodburner.

"Look at Old Blackie relax."
He said, "Isn't it wonderful
How relaxed a cat can get.
But...
Ready NOT to be!

22nd March 2008

Ghosts of Good Dogs

I feel a warm body
Pressed against my leg
Ghosts of good dogs gone

19th January 2012

Rapture

You have woken my soul from it's lonely sleep
You yearn me and churn me and make my heart leap
The thought of your love just fills me with flame
I go weak as a babe at the sound of your name

Rapture

Thank you and bless you, may you always be
As safe and secure as I'd want you to be
If I can't always be there, I want you to know
My love always folds round you with a warm loving glow

Rapture

I yearn to be with you, protecting and caring
Supporting and growing in loving and sharing
Come dance for me Lady, let our souls dance together
I promise to know you and love you forever

Rapture

1st January 2006

Morning Sun

The morning sun sets trees ablaze
With a fiery rosy tint,
It can do the same for days and days.
Without a carbon footprint

15th May 2008

Papaver Somniferum

Ahh Papaver Somniferum.
The fumes of long gone dreams,
A pipe or two and dreams of you
Are never what it seems!

This Blessed Balm from Heaven
Will sooth all kinds of pain,
But sad to say at the end of day
The pain doubles back again.

Better, soldier on regardless,
Than to take the easy way
But those dreams of yore, when you're feelin' sore
Will always make you pay

So like Old 'Tommy living cleanly'
Ignoring the horror of my fall
Now when I'm in pain, I say once again
I ONLY DREAM of Poppies growing tall.

10th February 2008

Cosmic Moorings

I know my place in time and space
My position in the human race

I've a good idea where I am going
And still, sometimes see where I'm growing

But sometimes now my heart is calling
Cast off from my cosmic mooring!

25th May 2010

My Ex-Wife

Your face
Sneering, scowling
Contorted with malice
Hands taloned to attack my face
If I remember you
It is like this
My wife.

My life
Has moved on from
Such sad and spiteful days
I suffered long enough for you
Now I'm free, rejoicing
Lib~er~at~ed
Reborn

I shall
Forgive, but not
For your sake but for mine
Forgiving sets me free, to be
Endlessly so grateful
To be away
From you

Now you
Cannot hurt me
You cannot hurt our son
We both grow beyond you, away
To replace your hateful
And selfish ways
With hope

And love
Beyond your ken
Feelings that are foreign
To your grim soul lost in darkness
We walk away, relieved
So free of you
At last!

20th March 2008

Meditations Of A Soldier

The following Poem contains violence and language that may be
offensive to some.
Please read/listen at your discretion.

You can see it coming,
A mile off,
On their hot,
Eager, unthinking, faces.
Always somewhere inappropriate.
Like a dinner-party.

"You were a soldier,"
"Did you …?"
"Have you ever …?"
Whispered… "Killed anybody?"
You want to reach out,
Across the table,
And bitch-slap 'em,
Back to reality.

How would you react,
If I were to reach,
Under the table,
And start to pile,
Upon our Hostess's
White table-cloth,
Body-parts?

Dead friends
And enemies,
And innocents.
Blood and faeces,
Splashing in your face,
Like this red wine
I symbolically flick
At you.

Do you really expect
An answer?
Do you think,
That we who went,

Were more fool than you?
Perhaps we were,
For going!
But don't assume
We still are.
We ALL offered
Service and Sacrifice,
Loyalty,
To Governments
Who proved unworthy
Of it.
Until the only loyalty
We felt was to
Each other,
Or to the dead.

What civilians do not realise
Is that the dead cannot hurt you.
It is always the living,
Who cause us problems.
All the dead can do
Is wake the live horror
In our minds
Of what man does to brother!
And what we have lost!

We learned to remember,
The friends and the fun,
The service and the hardship,
The lives that were saved!
Do you ever ask of them?
But we also learned,
To leave the killing
And the dying,
At the back-doors
Of our minds.

Lest it wake you,
And our hostess,
And fellow guests,
From their sleep,
As it still wakes us.
Occasionally.

Especially after
Your silly, thoughtless,
Idiot, questions!

So learn my friend,
That simplest of lessons,
One of the first,
That we as soldiers learned,
And keep your silly mouth
SHUT!

We have buried our dead,
And unless your name is
Jesus H. Christ,
It ain't your job
To resurrect 'em.
So ~ don't ~ f***ing ~
ASK!

11th March 2008

Jungle Warfare

Drifting through this hell of green
Trying to remain unseen
Youngsters really, many a teen
In a Jungle War e're their manhoods seen.
Just think what these kids might have been
While the dirty politicians preen.
You won't find them in this scene
'Cos they have to keep their hands clean!
Let's leave the kids in school with the Dean
And feed the politicians to the War Machine!

23rd May 2008

Ines

I saw that glance
As you looked back
Your eyes so brown
Your hair so black

Those perfect lips
A sculptor's dream
That oval face
Your skin like cream

Your hair like silk
Down that sweet back
I wish you'd looked
At me like that!

15th August 2009

Goodbye Charlton Heston

Goodbye Charlton Heston

I shall miss your acting skills
Your epic movies and the thrills

You may have been too fond of the gun
Or did it protect your place in the sun?
Surrender it now, this race is run!

To many you are the eternal charioteer
Now you're racing to a new frontier!

I know the Girls will miss you here.

13th April 2008

R.I.P Charlton Heston

Hunting

You ask me if I've hunted
Or been a fighter too,
Or if I'd leave the ladies,
So I say this to you.

Hunting, yes I've hunted
When I've needed to, to eat,
But never took much pleasure
In killing for my meat.

And soldiering, yes I've soldiered
When needed to, you must
When weaker trusting people
Need somebody they can trust.

But leave the ladies? Never!
I've no wish to lose touch
They can break a man or make him,
And I love 'em all too much!

And as for Mister Sun Tzu
My warring days are done
It's let's make love not war for me
Or, failing that ~ just RUN!

1st February 2008

Dawn's Rails Tanka

Pink tracks leading East
Beckon the early morning train
Rattling dawn-wards

Soon I shall ride those rails again
Until the wheels turn the pink to gold

20th April 2010

For My Heart

Give me Seaweed for my thyroid
Celery seed for gout,
Chilli and Ginger to warm my blood,
And Aspirin to thin it out.
Laughter for my spirit,
And Oh Dear God above
For my heart give me,
Love LoveLove

Give me food when I'm hungry
Give me water when I'm dry
Give me tasks my mind and hands can do
And Peace when I die.
Give me wisdom when I need it
Give me friends Dear God above
But for my heart give me
Love LoveLove

Give me companionship with animals
Give me tests to make me strong
A conscience when I need it
To save me from doing wrong
Give me kindness and understanding
And Oh Dear God above
For my heart give me
Love LoveLove

1st February 2008

Door

An exercise in surreal poetry

They say in Deep Space
No one can hear you scream!
Of course they can't,
There's no one there!

There is however, a door
A big, stout, solid door.

You never see it,
You never touch it,
Or hear it.

But you do hear
The echo of its slamming,
That tells you,
You are alone!

The echo,
Like a life,
Winking out!

19th February 2008

Dawn

Old man like me, I need my rest,
Three, maybe four hours at best,
But that puts my head just right,
Sleeping on the Black Breast of night.

When I leave my bed it is so neat
To put walking shoes upon my feet
Life greets me fresh each early morn
The amethyst nippled pink breast of dawn.

Oh what a way to start the day
Walking round the edge of Old Mount's Bay
Where Atlantic Current from Mexico
Meets the cold English Channel flow.

And to the East and overhead
Night's navy blue turns savage red,
And then the red to pink and blue
To greet another day so new.

This is the way I start my day
Whenever age and pain say I may,
And though I may be past my prime,
I'm getting younger all the time!

20th February 2008

Come My Darling

Come my darling. Hold me tight
Kiss me now and through the night,
To love so well will break no law
So kiss me now then kiss me more.

And while you undertake this task
There's just one thing that I ask
For now I want to kiss your back
And everywhere else, come to that!

There's a hunger in you I can feel
So no more armour, no more steel
I want to kiss each dip and swell
Each lovely breast and scar as well.

Let lips and fingers create desire
And stroke and stroke and stoke that fire,
So curling toes and bottom dance
And always always more romance.

Come lie with me and be my maid
In this battle you'll need no blade
There'll be no winner nor vanquish-ed
Just the glory of your bridal bed.

So come to me and be my sweet
I'll love you from your head to feet
I love you now and to your core
I'll love, love you, evermore.

12th December 2007

Breathing You In

I like the cool side of the pillow
The warm side of the bed
Your long slim legs entwined with mine
Your head beside my head.

My hand upon your belly
Your skin against my skin
And slowly pull you closer
And simply breathe you in!

Warm you feet upon me
Snuggle closer in
I'm glad to have you with me
And simply breathe you in!

20th January 2008

Boys and Girls

She Said
"You must be nine!"
In her
Chiding voice.
"Of course I am"
I replied
"You know the rules,
Boys WILL be boys!
But you girls
When you're awake
You are always
Grown-ups!"

18th January 2008

Boxes

When I
First moved into
This house I had a bed
And a rocking chair to my name
And boxes. About two
Hundred boxes
Of books

I told
A neighbour I
Was sitting on boxes
I was eating off boxes too
I was putting my feet
Up on boxes
Boxes

Two weeks
Later my new
Friend asked me if
I was still eating off boxes
"Not now" I said "Now I
Have a brand new
Dinner plate!"

27th March 2008

Book Shelves

Today
I have no time
For poetry and such
Today I must make bookcases
To make space for some of
This poetry
A~floor.

I'm tired
Of tripping up
On Kipling and Bukowski

And all of the Nav Works Bloggers
I will break my poor heart
For my poor art
Sometimes

But not
My neck, not yet
Not too young to die now
But en-tir-er-ly too busy
To pop my clogs over
A pile of books
Read and
Unread!

16th March 2008

Midwinter Solstice Tanka

Midwinter solstice
There is ice upon the ground
But the Jackdaw waits

When the sparrows leave the feeder
There will still be seed enough

~~~~~~~

Slipping adroitly
Between sunshine and showers
I walk the Beach Path

Sunlight warm against my neck
Avoiding icy puddles

22nd December 2009

Better Go Barefoot

Better to go barefoot
Than to wear that old soft shoe.
Be the altar of your own soul
And let them come and worship you!

You wear your torment and your pain
Like an old soft shoe
And so you live again, again
The things that damage you.

Upon their altars you lay you down
For them to cut and rend
Time to throw off the thorny crown
And change the pattern, Friend.

Take charge of your own journey
You are your only traffic cop.
You only do it over and over
Until the day you stop!

Better to go barefoot
Than wear that old soft shoe.
Build a brighter, lighter temple
And let them come and worship you!

13th February 2008

Spring Days Haiku

Oh for those Spring days
When my hair still grew curly
And my smile fitted

1st September 2012

Babycakes

Picture this.

Knock on the door
Postman
Parcel
Inscribed with my name
In full
No Mister
No Esquire
Just my name
Followed by
B.C.
Before Christ?

I wondered
I have sometimes
Been called
Old Man.
I enquired..
Earthy Mother
You've done it now
BABYCAKES! ! !
I knew I'd never
Live it down

25th January 2008

Evening Kestrel

Hovering above
The old Fishermen's Chapel
Evening's kestrel flight

1st September 2012

Bush Fire Tanka Chain

I remember smoke
On the wind, always warning
Of approaching fire

Out with the long handled shovel
And beat beatbeat all night

~~~~~~~

I have always said
You get one fire, you get more
There's always some fool

With more matches than sense
More paraffin than brain cells

~~~~~~~

The fire is beaten
And we see the damage done
All the loss of life

What better time to remember
Those friends that touched our hearts

8th December 2009

Kipling

Kipling, I loved him dearly
And in return
He tried to look like me

7th January 2012

Morphine New Year

I keep hearing of a White Christmas
Filled up with such Love and such cheer
But between the pain and the fears, the loss and the tears
What colour is a morphine new year?

To those of us to whom Merry Christmas
Means a comrade in bits here and there
Or the girl we would date who just wouldn't wait
What colour is a morphine new year?

Don't get me wrong the Christmas we fought for
Was often the one you hold dear
But we gave all we could, often more than we should
What colour is a morphine new year?

To those of us to whom Merry Christmas
Means a comrade in bits here and there
Or the girl we would date who just wouldn't wait
What colour is a morphine new year?

I remember Christmas in the Jungle
Weighted down with weapons and gear
But shrapnel will floor and the bayonet will gore
What colour then a morphine new year

And that was the way it started
After the wound and the fear
A thump and a sigh, a syrette in the thigh
Started many a morphine new year

We did what we had to as needed
And we usually did it with good cheer
But after forty five years of much pain and tears
I still fight for the right to a CHAIR!*

And now after thirty years drug free
I'm back where I started I fear
I thank you so much for the Christmas
I just didn't want the morphine new year!

So now the battle starts over

To be rid of this chemical curse
If only they'd given me poppy
Instead of these inventions much worse!

So I know you want Christmas all fluffy
All white with tinselly airs
It's so rude to ask, but I need help with my task
What colour is a morphine new year?

6th January 2010

This is just a reminder that while we still send our young men off to war it can make Christmas mean something entirely different to those who lose loved ones or their health over this so called period of peace and goodwill!

Despite being in chronic pain a lot of the time I seldom resort to pain killers any more but for 15 days over the end of December '09 and January '10 I was forced to use morphine again after 30 years off it. You can probably gather that I wasn't happy about it! I am pleased to report that, so far, I have not had to resort to it again!

*My reference to fighting for the right to a CHAIR refers to the fact that despite being an 80% disabled Veteran I've just been told that the application for a assessment for an orthorpedic chair that I made in 2003 has been lost and that I must now apply for an assessment again. Estimated waiting period for assessment = 1 year!

Haiku and Pictures

Patiently we stand
Like a monument to time
Enduring ~ Granite

~~~~~

Ancient beech woods shine
Light and shade ~ mossy boulders
Listen to leaves fall

23rd April 2010

Life And Death In The Forest

When darkness settles
And the wind forgets to blow
The trees are silent

But no matter how quiet
The bamboo always rustles

~~~~~

So quiet she lies
Stretched upon her leafy bed
Resting in the sun

A monument to her life
A Greater Serenity

26th April 2010

Beech Wood Haiku

Evening sun shines
Sideways through the trees ~ bird song
Calling all to rest
These old beech woods wait
For the joyful sound of pigs
Autumn's mast rights feast

30th April 2010

Mast rights were the rights of the medieval peasants to turn their stock
out in the forest to forage for mast, an early English name for tree seed,
namely beech, sweet chestnut and oak mast. This was in essence free
feed just at the time when stock needed fattening up for winter, or the
larder. This must have been a joyous time for the stock and the peasant
families. I often think I can almost hear the echo of contented stock
foraging in the woods. I wonder if the woods can remember them. Res

Penzance Harbour Winter Tanka

Packed in together
Cheek by jowl and stem to stern
Hiding from the storms

Praying for a safe mooring
Wishing for better weather
And in the water

Still looking for safe harbour
Are those whose search failed
Now washed by an angry sea

Lying where the storm found them

4th May 2010

Farewell Haiku

Little Church nestling
Beside the River Camel
Sweet morning birdsong

Blackbird sings on graves
St Michael's Church Porthilly
Mother's favourite song

14th May 2010

History

In Olden Days which are best forgotten,
The men were hard and the times were rotten.
In Saint Buryan, there did dwell
A brawny farmer, I knew him well.

Henwood Penwallet, take my word
Grew the finest shallots, in the Western World.
Those times being hard, he did say,
"I'll take a load to sell up England way!"

'Course, silly bugger, didn't know the way,
So he followed the coast line, every day.
Suddenly he found, before he could scoot,
An English Army camped across his route.

He thought he'd try to sell them shallot
But conscripted was all he got.
They thought perhaps he was a Yeoman
So they turned him into a bowman.

The King before the battle visited his men,
And gave 'em peppy speeches to make 'em brave again
He checked the lances sharpened, the axes fit to slice
And then he came to Henwood, 'an spoke to him so nice.

"You any good with that bow?" he asked, "My good man."
"Buggered if I know, I'm a conscript, that's what I am!"
"Well, try it out, see if you can hit that tree o'er there."
The arrow flew, left and right and vanished in the air!

King Harold said, "Don't worry, you're doin' fine!"
"Captain, put this Cornishman in the front line.
An' for Gods sake!" he said, "Have someone watch that prat,
He'll have someone's eye out, shooting arrows like that!"

Hastings 1066
17th March 2008

My Morning Began 3 Tanka

My morning began
Hunting for the Early Worm
Fuel for my life

It's a well fed blackbird sings
The most exquisite love songs

My morning began
Stealing that which was not mine
This is my nature

The Divine Hand that made me
Bade me thrive ~ so I obey

My morning began
Taking bluebells to Mother
Maybe for the last time

However ~ the less I come
The closer our next meeting

11th May 2010

My IT Consultant

I have an IT Consultant
Who gently, with words of one syllable,
Patiently leads me through the complexities
Of Mobiles, landlines, filters,
Modems, USB's and other such mysteries.
Whose gentle voice sometimes pauses
Just long enough, for me to say
I love you!

28th January 2008

63

Lao Tzu

Confucius he say:-
"Given a few more years
Of life to finish my study
Of the Book of Changes,
And I may be free from great errors!"

Just goes to show
What a Big-head,
Confucius was!

Lao Tzu smiled
And whispered:-
"The beginning of all things,
Lies still in the beyond,
In the form of ideas,
Yet to become real."

We both smiled
And walked on,
Arm in arm,
Playing Ping-Pong,
With ideas of Love.

Xiao Gao Jiao, Little Longhorn,
Munched contentedly,
On fresh grass and water chestnuts,
I'd gathered for him.
Kind brown eyes liquid,
With loving wisdom,
Too slow and deep
For me to understand.

"When will you get to the West,
Master?" I asked,
"When can I expect to see you
Riding down Causwayhead in Penzance,
On your water buffalo."

The Old Man smiled,
Put a finger to his lips,
"Ah you Westerners," he said fondly,

"Better to live in wonder
Than just wondering!"

With a twinkle in his eye,
He squeezed my arm and said,
"Little Brother, if you thought less
And felt more, you'd know,
I'm already there with you!"

20th February 2008

Comments in italics:-

Confucious's statement is from his "Analects"
Lao Tzu's statement is from the "I Ching"

Reflections

The window reflects
Dove and sparrows eating grain
Busier than I

They eat the seed I buy ~ but
I have the best of the deal

0h the mirror reflects
My own face but much older
There is something wrong

Why can't it portray my face
Without showing the sorrow

18th May 2010

Asked Mother

"These are your playmates?" asked Mother.

Eyeing the East End kids
On the TB ward, warily!
"Why, they talk like gutter-snipes.
Not our sort of people at all!"

"Yeah, they're me mates!" said I
In the language of my peers
"But why don't you touch me?
Why don't you hold me?
Why don't you kiss me?
Said I, aged four, strapped flat on my back

"Woz that yer 'Olds'?"
Asked the East End kids
With the kindness of the streets
"But why don't they touch you?
Why don't they kiss you?
Why don't they bring you bread and dripping?"

"These are your friends?" asked Mother.
When she saw my travelling companions.
"Why they are almost like gypsies,
Not our sort of people at all!"

"That was your family?"
My friends asked, those
Men of the travelling people
"Why don't they touch you?
Why don't they hold you?
Why don't they kiss you?
Why don't they care for you?"

"Come sit down by the fire.
Take tay or take a drink,
Break bread, taste salt.
Come listen to some tales
Which will touch you,
Which will hold you,
And which will kiss your soul!"

"These are your workmates?" asked Mother.
Eyeing Jim Keating and Tony Barry
From Ennis in County Clare
"Why, they are almost gypsies,
Not our sort of people at all!"

"Was that your family?"
My travelling Irish friends said.
"Why did they not touch you?
Why did they not hold you?
Why did they not kiss you?
Why did they not care for you?"

"Come sit down by the fire
You've earned your bread today
By the sweat of your brow
And the strain on your back
You've earned your beer
And you've earned your tack
Come sing up a song
That will touch you
That will hold you
That will kiss your soul!"

"These are your friends, Dear?" said Mother.
Looking through the Photo Album
"Why, they look quite foreign,
Why are they nearly naked?
Why, they look like savages!
Not our sort of people at all!"

"You are a long way from your family."
Said my Head-hunter friends.
"With no one to touch you,
No one to hold you,
No one to kiss you,
You must feel so alone!"

"So come sit down by the fire
Here's some rice wine for joy.
Sing us a song, share in our dance,
Here's the young maiden who captured your glance
She's young and she's lovely

And she loves your white skin,
She will touch you,
She will hold you,
And she will kiss your soul!"

So these are my friends, Mother,
And they've done me no end of good
And had you, like me, joined them for tea
They'd have done you no end of good too.

I hope where you've gone to now, Mother.
You have learned to see a bit clear,
That the men of the earth are the salt of the earth
And the one's who are worth holding dear.

And I hope where you've gone to now, Mother.
You can find someone to hold dear,
Who will touch you,
And who will hold you,
And maybe, kiss your soul!

20th May 2010

Monkey See...

Monkey see
Monkey do
Monkey bite

1st January 2012

Snake Screamer

Monkey on the fence
Lived in an Anchor Beer crate
Sweet thing ~ Snake screamer

25th August 2012

Dreams of Portobello

You're schlepping down to Portobello
When Portobello was THE Scene
And you're young enough to cut it
And too old to be too green

You've got a little swagger
You know you're lookin' good
An' you've got a dangle going
And it's riding like it should

So you catch the ladies glances
And you're nimble on your feet
And you're known on every corner
As a cool dude on the street

The straightest dealer on the block
Delivers to your home
Hand rubbed hash or best Thai sticks
You seldom smoke alone

*Leonard drops in for a chat
To see what he can discover
I wonder how many spliffs got rolled
On his first two LP covers?

*He passes Cat Stevens on his way
He has the flat above
And the most beautiful call girls in the world
Sell their surrogated love

You can drop into Hennessey's
For a drink with all the boys
Hawkwind's drummer buys you a pint
Says, "Sorry about the noise!"

You can grab a pint at Finche's
Or a curry at East and West
But for Peas and Rice the proper way
The Mangrove is the best

You can meet up with a travelin' friend

Just hitch-hiked back from Thailand
Or spend the night with those Aussie Girls
You met out in the Islands

You can schlepp on down to Notting Dale
Find Bob Squire making tea
Him 'n' John Martyn playin' crib
And Beverley bored as can be

Bob always telling Vernon
"Don't you bring the Old Bill near!"
And when Old Bill did come round
Bob said, "He don't live 'ere!"

But that was in the good old days
When Dear Juttè was still living
When Bermuda Mick would cut a dash
Before Martin took to drinking

When Kieth and Val were host to all
Their tiny room a-popping
And Andy was quite beautiful
And the whole joint was a-rockin'

I still listen for that other beat
That I used to use for walkin'
But I think now it is Time's feet
And It's me that He is stalking

And now it seems just like a dream
My loves 'n' friends of yesteryear
But if you can remember it
They say you were not there!

29th May 2010

*Verses ma with an * refer to Mayfair, where I worked, not the area of North Kensington that included Notting Hill, Portobello Road and Ladbroke Grove where I lived.

Shlepping ~ from Yiddish ~ To walk laboriously, but as adopted into London slang it meant to walk with style, panache.

Old Bill ~ Police

Love to all ~ Res

Sea Salt

Here in Cornwall, where I reside,
We live with sea, we live with tide
The English Channel brings the cold
The Great Atlantic, wild and bold.
Both these seas surround us here
Where 'ere we go, the sea is near.

Sometimes pacific, almost benign,
But always waiting for its time!
Artists love it, come to see
The blue, the green, the turquoise sea.
But we who live here, all the time
We never trust that sea sublime.

Oh, she can change from blue so rich
To wicked, murderous, killing bitch!
And when the wind's behind the scend
She'll take ship and man, to their salty end!
Ship killer! Man eater! Child stealer, she be!
Bringing us "Nearer My God To Thee!"

Yet men who sail out there so brave
Upon her bosom, upon her wave,
They bring the food, they bring the trade,
Were ever greater heroes made?
They love her still and their life so free
Making their Daily Bread upon the sea

22nd March 2008.

Liam Clancy, RIP

God rest ye, Liam Clancy
You were a lovely boy
With magic in your music
And a way of spreading joy.

God rest ye, Liam Clancy
A true son of Erin's Isle
Your voice could break a thousand hearts
Or make a Nation smile!

God rest ye, Liam Clancy
The music was your own
I pray your Mercy Angels
Will carry you safely home.

God rest ye, Liam Clancy
I'll shed a lonely tear
We're poorer for you passing
But richer you were here!

God rest ye, Liam Clancy
Your music will not pass
And while I play your songs again
I'll raise a Parting Glass.

Rest Well, Old Friend

5th December 2009

Blades

I am the sword of the Samurai,
Lovingly sharpened , honed,
Polished by skilled craftsman's hands.
Some talk of thirsty blades,
But we are indifferent to flesh.
Though flesh is unwise to cross us!

I am the Cavalry Sabre,
Sharpened on the mobile whetstone,
Every unit carries, before battle.
I am the pike and the bayonet,
The shining spear point blade,
Winking in the sun and air.

I am myriads of knives
Fighting, hunting, whittling
Cooking but seldom "Flick".
Invariably an inferior tool,
Made from suspect steel.
And wielded by fools.

I am the carpenters chisel.
Honed bright on Arkansas Stone,
And leather or canvas strop.
Handle polished smooth with use,
Fit to pare wood thinner than a whisker
Worthy of the hand of a Saviour.

I am the surgeon's scalpel,
Razor sharp, stainless,
Used only once.
And I am millions of razors,
Open, safety, twin, three, four, five
Bladed and disposable.

Scraping daily at men's chins
And ladies legs, etcetera.
I am carbon enriched steel
Danish, Solingen, Damascus.
Forged in the white heat
Of the furnace glare.

I am Scorpio personified,
As good or evil as he who uses it,
As constructive or destructive,
The Sharp Cutting Edge.

26rh March 2008

Odes to Caroline

She loved red roses
Champagne and best white cocaine
And she loved to dance

She'd make love like no tomorrow
And died dancing ~ yesterday

~~~~~~~~~~~~~~~~~~~~~~

Caroline
~~~~~

You were a wild child
Like a banquet, feasting life
Beauty dancing past.

Are you somewhere still?
Cooking wonderful food, that smile
Heavenly sunshine.

You were the whirlwind
Or a star brightly burning
In-can-des-cent-ly.

You lived three lifetimes
With your lust for adventure
Gone now, Carolina.

Still loved and still missed
There hasn't been a party
Like your last, last dance.

18th June 2010

Campfire Dreams

A Tanka Chain

Tribal voices call
Uniting all the People
The beat of the drum

Synchronising the heart beat
As Brother and Sister meet
*

I saw you dancing
Such grace, such feminine poise
Like a slender spruce

Waving in the mountain wind
My soul melted into yours
*
I watched the fire light
Anoint your silken shoulder
Where I longed to kiss

Every curve and sway held me
Captive ~ burning in the flames
*
Come dance with me now
Until the drums fall silent
And the music dies

But we and the flames still dance
With our two hearts intertwined

24th June 2010

Trees

I love wood
I love the touch
And the smell of it
I love the textures
All different

From the long grained
Knotless Piranha Pine
To the dense wriggles
Of Ancient Yew
Long fibred Sitka
And the silica sparks
Of Bloodwood Satine

The midnight shine
Of Andaman Ebony
The visual delights
Of all the Rosewoods
To the perfume of
The sugars boiling off
Turning apple.

I love it fresh from sharp steel
With a shine all of its own
Or sanded by finer and finer paper
Or emery, wet and dry
Until the surface glows
Like warm glass.

I love the things
You can make
Books
And bookcases
To keep them on.

Plates bowls spoons vases
Cups chopsticks
Rollers for mangles
Wheels to carry your loads
And carts to carry your families
And beds for you all to sleep on.

Handles for tools
Elm water pipes
That last from Roman times
To the present day.

Wooden boats to sail the sea
And bring back more wood
Exciting and exotic woods
That smell like spices!

But most of all
I love the trees!
We have taken enough
From the forest!
If we are not willing
To nurture the seedlings
Clear the weeds
Dig the soil
And cherish the saplings
Then leave the trees alone!

So take your axe and chainsaw
And beat them into
Trowels and
Straight Planting Spades.

If you wish to use the bounty
Of the forest
First plant your trees
And sometimes, during your labours
Rest in the shade of your trees
And in these days of Global Warming
You will learn how trees
Cool the air!

Learn the secrets of the woods
And jungles
Learn to love them
Before you claim the right
To use them!

And you, human?
In your suit and white cuffs

Hiding behind the tree
You have no business
In the woods
Take off your choking ties
Your manufacture
Your profit and loss
Your futures trading
Away!
Off the Tree!
You have no business here!

Leave the trees to breathe
Let them get on with the business
Of making more trees
Manufacturing topsoil
Stabilising mountainsides
Fixing nitrogen from the air
Into the soil around their roots.

Holding rainfall in the ground
To feed the forest and the streams
That all Earths' Children may drink
Without flood or erosion.

Leave the trees to breathe
To filter dust and gasses
From the air
So that our children and grandchildren
May also breathe.
Leave the trees to heal
The damage that you, human
Have done!

BEFORE IT IS TOO LATE!

30th June 2010

The Legend of Port Quin

I see your pale face at the small cottage window
Your sad eyes always looking far over the sea
Searching the skyline for the fishing boats coming
But there'll be no more homecomings for you and for me.

Every man in the village was out for the fishing
Every boat in the village was out on the sea
When the weather came storming in from the nor' west
Now there'll be no more homecomings for you and for me.

Grandfathers, Fathers and their sons now just learning
The hard ways of fishing and working the sea
In one short afternoon, so suddenly taken
So there'll be no more homecomings for you and for me.

Every man in the village so suddenly drown-ded
Every wife, every girl now a widow must be
And now every small cottage window is suddenly tear stained
There'll be no more homecomings for you and for me.

I was young and was strong and was happily married
My young wife would sing her sweet love songs to me
Now I see her in black in the small tear stained window
There'll be no more homecomings for I'm lost at sea.

I see your pale face at the small cottage window
Your sad eyes still looking far over the sea
For three hundred years still searching the horizon
But there'll be no more homecomings for you and for me.

I've watched as the slates from the roofs began slipping
Watched as the weeds grew where we played happily
But still I see your dear face in the small tear stained window
As I watch from my berth here in the stormy grey sea.
(Fading)
There'll be no more homecomings for you and for me.
No scones by the fire as you pour me my tea
No singing me love songs as you sit on my knee
There's no more homecomings for you and for me.

26th August 2010.

I wrote this after hearing about the Legend of Port Quin. The legend goes that in 1698 all the men of Port Quin were drowned in a storm that sprang up suddenly one afternoon while they were fishing. All the women of the small village were left widowed or orphaned and had to move away because without any men to fish, the village starved. Port Quin was left abandoned.

Forked Tongues Tanka

It is morning and
I have had no sleep... but still
The sparrows chatter

Do they speak the truth... d'you think
Or do they speak with forked tongues

7th September 2010

Seagull Sentries

The first light of day
Steals quietly through the town
Seagull sentries watch

19th September 2012

Old Singapore

In Old Singapore
I used to love Thousand Year Eggs
So long as they were fresh

September 2012

Brown-Bread Tommy

Poor Tommy Atkins
In trouble
Running round the square
"Double!
"Large pack small pack
Bayonet and scabbard
Bullet pouches all
Buckled upon him.
Rifle overhead
At full stretch
Of his puny arms.

Sergeant Ottley
Drill Sergeant
Or as we said
Drill Pig!
The scourge of the innocent!
Fault finder among the faultless!
The only person
In the British Army,
Certified :-
"Unfit for Human Consumption!"
Pursuing him
With demented shrieks
"Double, double!
Lift that rifle up!
Higher, higher!
Get them knees up!
Higher, higher!"

Poor Tommy demised.
Run into the ground!
Brown-bread,
Dead!
Passed over!
Answered the final question!
Gone for a Burton!
D/D,
Discharged /Dead!

Poor Tommy
After he'd handed back
His rifle and kit
He was posted To Heaven.
Saint Peter said
"Welcome,
You are welcome here
Because you knew hell
On earth."

Crafty Tommy
Peeked in the Gates
Recoiled!
And shuddered!
Up on the throne
Starched and polished
Chevroned and straight!
Ottley!
"I'm not comin' in there!"
Sez Tommy,
"That's Sergeant Ottley!"

"No No!"
Saint Peter cried,
"You'll be alright.
That's not Ottley,
That's God!
He just thinks he's Ottley!

29th March 2008

Green Velvet

She wore a green velvet
Evening gown... all dressed up
And ready to dance

19th September 2012

Today's Haiku

An old brass bedstead
Grown into a ragged fence
Polished by sparrows

~~~~~~~~~~~~~~~~~~~~~~

In a dry grass bed
Under the brambles... snoring
A nest of Dormice

~~~~~~~~~~~~~~~~~~~~~~

Hidden in the hedge
An old enamel tea pot
A nest for a wren

~~~~~~~~~~~~~~~~~~~~~~

On a barbed wire fence
Insects impaled on the spikes
A Shrike's full larder

~~~~~~~~~~~~~~~~~~~~~~

Caught in the barb wire
A tuft of sheep's wool.... soft white
Lining for birds nests

~~~~~~~~~~~~~~~~~~~~~~

Found in the chimney
Woven in a Jackdaw's nest
Child's pink sun glasses

~~~~~~~~~~~~~~~~~~~~~~

Red hair in the wire
Plotting a map in my mind
Brother Fox's path

3rd March 2011

Pencil Haiku"

Sometimes I think
A nice sharp pencil point'll
Prod my muse to work

14th March 2011

A Walk Around The Fields Of My Mind

Haiku

Tires swish on wet roads
No smell of the earth drinking
Missing the woodlands
~~~~~~~~~~~~~~~~~~~~~~

She rubs against me
Like an affectionate cat
Half a ton of bovine love
~~~~~~~~~~~~~~~~~~~~~~~

Some years The blackthorn blossom
Lies like snow
Upon the branch
~~~~~~~~~~~~~~~~~~~~~~

Hawthorn blossom
Seldom heard
Over the sound of casting clouts
~~~~~~~~~~~~~~~~~~~~~~~~~~~~

Gathering
Sticky buds in the grave yard
Balm of Gilead
~~~~~~~~~~~~~~~

A Vixen's love song
Is not a thing of beauty
'Cept to a dog fox
~~~~~~~~~~~~~~~~~

The smell of sweet sap
Rising from the saw's sharp blade
Next winter's firewood
~~~~~~~~~~~~~~~~~~~~~~~~

Sitting underneath
A flowering cherry tree
Basho fills my mind
~~~~~~~~~~~~~~~~~~~~

Sea breezes jangle
The wind chimes made of sea shells
In the life guard's hut

Winter ploughing
With a great long white kite tail
Of following seagulls

A shepherd's reward
After days and nights of toil
Spring lambs

Beach combing was so
Much nicer in early days
Before the plastic bottle

4th March 2011

Paddy

(That's short for Patricia, not one of my Irish friends)

Our parting tears
Yours and mine
I gathered in
A blue paisley
Handkerchief.
I rolled it tightly
And sewed it shut
Tight, neat, little
Stitches,
And tried to forget

I joined the Army
To forget.
Because I couldn't
Speak French
And a daily ration
Of rough sour wine

Didn't interest me.
But climbing mountains
Did. Canoeing
Rivers did!

Years later,
Mountains and
Valleys later.
Loves later,
Service and wounds later.
Captivities and Freedoms later,
Sacrifice and rebirths later,
I found the handkerchief
And that little wooden mouse
In my folk's attic,
Among other dusty traces
Of vanished youth.

I cut the stitches,
and unrolled the handkerchief.
The tears were
No longer there.

Now fifty years
Later. The pain
Has gone. Even
The longing.

But perhaps
Like a faded spot
On an old tear stained handkerchief
There is a trace,
Just a shadow,
Of regret,
At what we missed,
At what we might have been.
But your memory warms
My old heart. Thank you.
Fare thee well!

6th March 2011

Five Haiku for Sarawak

My old sarong fades
But memory still calls me
Rice wine 'neath the skulls

Down in the longhouse
Ghosts dangle from the rafters
Join in every song

Chinese New Year cards
From Borneo and Johore
Kitchen God smiles down

Kuching... friendly town
Known for its lovely women
And Oh.... mee hoon soup

Bau... known for its gold
Pretty girls with dimpled cheeks
All those friendly smiles

8th March 2011

Dark Streets

In the dark wet streets
High heels ring on paving stones
Dark blind windows watch

Tired heads on pillows
Stir and listen for a while
Beauty tripping past

19th September 2012

Our Billy and Me

"Our Billy and Me"
Her affection still lives on
In sepia dreams

19th September 2012

Inspiration from a photo borrowed from Spitalfields Life. With sincere thanks to my dear friend Jackie Siess for the inspiration. Thanks Essex Girl

The Last Rickshaw Man

Carrying flowers
Past Old Kuching's Courthouse
Her last Rickshaw Man

He liked the flowers
"All those people heavier
And smell worse," he smiled

19th September 2012

Japanese Earthquake Haiku

I hear from Vancouver
Of Tokyo quakes... small world
In peril

Sitting safe at home
My heart goes out to all at risk
In quaking Tokyo

Man is so small
When the Dragon shrugs it's shoulders
Playthings of the Gods

Japan lies bleeding
Scattered across her farm land
My heart bleeds for her

Ships take to the land
And cars take to the water
Racing to destruction

After the quake... the waves
So many lives turned upside down
Reduced to mud and matchsticks

Every child I see
Rescued, saved from the wreckage
My heart swells... tearful joy

I see the loving care
As a boat load of children
Are passed hand to hand

Save them all... Dear God
Or Goddess... save all of them
They need your mercy now

Our thoughts and prayers
Are with you all in Japan
Living in harm's way

11th March 2011

I was up early listening on line to Duke Lang's "Better Days" Radio
Programme from Vancouver when we first heard of Japan's terrible
earthquake and tsunami on 11th March 2011. Duke had a listener in
Tokyo who kept us updated during the programme. Some of this was
written as it was happening and some later after more news was
received.

The Sands of Time Ode to John Betjeman

Written for a Poetry Challenge. The challenge was to write a poem
including sand dunes without mentioning either word, this was the
result.

Take the train to Bodmin Road
They call it Parkway now
But little has changed
Except the sign.

Catch the bus to Padstow
Rattling and shaking
Through the Cornish
Countryside.

Did you know Cornish Drivers
Can drive as fast backwards
As forwards
Narrow lanes teach backing
Fast.

Padstow or Padstein
As they call it now
Fish smell from the harbour
Gulls call, all the time
Buy a flower!
Not a kiss me quick hat.

Look across the Camel
That's a River not a cigarette
D'you see Brae Hill
Standing huge, rounded
Beach heaped by the wind.

Partly grass covered, tufty
Blown detritus
Of the River
Estuary. Take the ferry
Go there.

The far side of Brae Hill
Is part of a golf course

And the hill becomes
The largest bunker in the world.

Unless you count Saudi
Which is of course
All bunker
What ain't concrete
Or hotels
Now.

Walk across the Golf Course
Beware of low flying balls!
Mostly grass but granular ground
Showing here and there.

Beyond the greens like velvet
You'll find a little church
Tiny, once lost under
The flying wind blown
Grains of beach.

Walk through the hedge
Of tamarisk, look right
First grave you see
Lay your flower down.

Dear Sweet Poet
I hope the granular
Open grained, porous
Nature of your bed
Allows the songs to filter
Down to you there.

The song of the Sea
Beating upon Doom Bar
And the wind in the tamarisk
The song of Trebetherick
Which you loved so well
And the song I would sing to thee
Had I the sweet facility
You had with words.

Rest in Peace
John Betjeman
"Poet and Hack"
Poet Laureate
Social Climber and Knight
And lover of
Miss J Hunter Dunn.

You lie among these tiny
Wind polished grains
Of Daymer Bay
Like myriads of universes
Ground small by time
And the tide.

22nd February 2008

Ancient Visions

An elderly gentleman
Standing in the middle of the junction
Completely oblivious to the traffic
Trying to edge around him.

I took him by the elbow
And led him to the safety of the kerb.

"D'you know?" he said wistfully
Gazing at the mist haloed street lights,
"It was just such an evening as this
I last saw Nonie Collins!"

30th March 2011

I must confess that I was the elderly gentleman and the passerby who
led him to the kerb!

Country Memories Haiku

New born foal - too weak
And tall to suckle with ease
Bonds with my sweater

Newly born goat kids
Agility in goatskin
Running the ridgepole

Goats up in a tree
View pedestrians with scorn
"We don't graze, we browse!"

Cold frosty morning
Breath hangs like smoke on the air
Mucking out calf pens

4th May 2011

November Scribblings

My cottage lay
In the shadow of Carn Brae
Last hill in England

The bus drivers knew
My bus stop....the third gorse bush
After Henwood's haystack

Dead fox hill
So steep, so straight, so fast
Reynard's bane

Two dogs... five fields over
Waiting for the school bus
My boy's welcome home

The flooded clay-pit
Where the post-man drowned himself
Our summer playground

Our horizon was dark
Until distant St Buryan
Got its first street light

Six miles from the sea
But when the Sou-Westerlies blew
Salt on our lips and windows

The weeping willow
Trailing its many fingers
In the passing stream

Headache?
Chew some willow bark
Nature's aspirin

1st December 2011

More Memories of Rural Life

Lobo, good boy's dog
Towing my son up and down
The flooded clay-pit

Lobo, water dog
Only her head showing
Surrounded by shiver ripples

Happiness for a boy
His very own dog
And a litter of puppies
We had a great zip line
Something for the kids to play on
Health and Safety… moi?

By January
Even a flooded hoof print
Would be full of frog spawn

There were wild orchids
Growing in the summer grass
Protecting thousands of tiny frogs

Guy Fawks night bonfires
A year's brush-wood up in smoke
The guy, a witch, a dragon, a masterpiece

3rd December 2011

Donkey Tales

Donkey in the kitchen
With her hungry face on
Rattling the lid of the bread bin

My boy and his donkey
Busy with the daily round
Two hearts intertwined

My boy and his donkey
And a smart little two wheeled shay
A chick magnet country style

Donkey and cart
Rattling down the main road
Surf-boards on the back

Blanket on the beach
Donkey in the middle of it
"Where's my sandwich?"

Stop at a road-side café
Ruan, donkey and I
Pot of tea for three

Donkey at the fair
Giving rides to the kids
Fuelled by Saffron Cakes

The donkey cart
Full of ropes and climbing harness
Off collecting tree seeds

My son and I collecting seed
Seventy feet up a western hemlock
The donkey waits below

Donkey back in the field
With two Arab race-horses
Donkey rules the roost

3rd December 2011

Village Life
(Almost Any Village in South East Asia)

The children sit
On the back of the water buffalo
Who is minding who?

The women sing
Rice planting songs
Knee deep in cool water

In the bird scarer's hut
The babies sleep
Hanging in sarong hammocks

The planting done
A little gift of food and flowers
At the village shrine

The men drain the paddy
For the sun to warm the roots
Then flood again… the ageless cycle

When ripe the rice is harvested
Threshed and winnowed
There is no prosperity like a full granary

A harvest festival
A toddler is lost in the crowd
Found curled up safe with the water buffalo

14th January 2012

Andy Jolley

Yesterday I sat
Where Neville Shute's father prayed
In that little church at Egloshale
I wonder if he imagined
His son's words would fly around the world
Just as his son did
Uniting Cornwall with Dublin
With Burma and Malaya
And his beloved Australia
And who was
Just like my nephew Andy
Another of Wadebridge's best loved sons

4th January 2012

R.I.P. Andy Jolley 1967 - 2011

Hell Bank Notes

Hell Bank Notes
The afterlife taken care of
Now what about this one

Burning Hell Bank Notes
I'll be a rich man when I'm dead
Think I'll burn some girls now

Don't panic ladies, only paper ones, honest!

18th September 2012

Please Don't 'Go' Here

Some places are just
No Go areas ~ so there
So please don't 'Go' here

18th September 2012

Wild Geese

Flight of the Wild Geese
That small nations might be free
Proud tears of Erin

17th September 2012

Vote Rope

Did they promise us
A hung parliament... or
Not... wishful thinking?
Perhaps they'll vote another
Allowance... this time for hemp!

21.5.2010

This isn't as bloodthirsty as it looks. Just a satirical take on all the predictions of a 'hung parliament' and all the Members of Parliament who were caught inflating their Allowance Claims!

Dry Earth

Feet tread the dry earth
Eyes search the sky for rain clouds
As his fathers did

18th September 2012

Tiger Balm Gardens

Tiger Balm Gardens
One captured glance from long ago
Still makes my heart quake

16th September 2012

Seagull

Seagull
Like a flying handkerchief
Blown across the bay

20th August 201

Stapling Rocks

Here in Cornwall
We get such weather
We often staple
Rocks together!

To make our sea wall
Strong and stout
To keep the tide
And water out.

But sea salt and iron
You can trust
Eventually will
Give way to rust!

So now when our sea wall
We must heal
We put our trust in
Stainless steel!

9th May 2008

Monterey Pines and Cypresses

Pines and cypresses
All the way from Monterey
Thrive in Cornish soil

13th September 2012

Monsoon Water

Monsoon water rising
Cipher machines up on bricks
A canoe ride home

16th September 2012

Buck Polly

Buck Polly my friend
Another twelve stringer down
The needle of death

18th September 2012

Bert Jansch wrote a poignant song about Buck's death entitled "Needle of Death"R.I.P. Buck Polly.

Moon

The moon crept in
On bare feet ~ to whisper
Secrets in my dreams

18th September 2012

Index

MAPublisher Catalogue

ISBN/Titles /Image/Author	ISBN/Titles /Image/Author	ISBN/Titles /Image/Author	ISBN/Titles /Image/Author
978-1-910499-00-9 Father to child By Mayar Akash	978-1-910499-08-5 HSJ Lakri Tura By Mayar Akash	978-1-910499-26-9 Colouring 1-10 By MAPublisher	978-1-910499-18-4 Basic Numbers 1-10 By MAPublisher
978-1-910499-16-0 River of Life By Mayar Akash	978-1-910499-09-2 HSJ Gilaf Procession By Mayar Akash	978-1-910499-27-6 Activity Numbers 1-10 By MAPublisher	978-1-910499-19-1 Number 1-100 By MAPublisher
978-1-910499-39-9 Eyewithin By Mayar Akash	978-1-910499-03-0 HSJ Mazar Sharif By Mayar Akash	978-1-910499-28-3 Activity Colouring Alphabets By MAPublisher	978-1-910499-20-7 Vowels By MAPublisher
978-1-910499-32-0 WG Survivor By Mayar Akash	978-1-910499-06-1 Hazrat Shahjalal By Mayar Akash	978-1-910499-68-9 The Adventures of Sylheti mazars By Mayar Akash	978-1-910499-21-4 Alphabet Consonants By MAPublisher
978-1-910499-66-5 Yesteryears By Mayar Akash	978-1-910499-07-8 HSJ Urus By Mayar Akash	978-1-910499-38-2 Bite Size Islam: 99 Names of Allah By Mayar Akash	978-1-910499-22-1 Vowels & Short By MAPublisher

ISBN/Titles /Image/Author	ISBN/Titles /Image/Author	ISBN/Titles /Image/Author	ISBN/Titles /Image/Author
978-1-910499-15-3 Anthology One By Penny Authors	978-1-910499-36-8 Delirious By Liam Newton	978-1-910499-52-8 Lit From Within By Ruth Lewarne	978-1-910499-57-3 The Vampire of the Resistance By Ruth Lewarne
978-1-910499-17-7 Anthology Two By Penny Authors	978-1-910499-54-2 Book of Lived v6 Penny Authors	978-1-910499-49-8 Cry for Help By B. M. Gandhi	978-1-910499-55-9 Riversolde By Meriyon
978-1-910499-29-0 Book of Lived v3 By Penny Authors	978-1-910499-37-5 When You Look Back By Rashma Mehta	978-1-910499-14-6 The Halloweeen Poem by Zainab Khan	978-1-910499-70-2 Smiley & The Acorn By Roger Underwood
978-1-910499-351 V4 Book of Lived By Penny Authors	978-1-910499-37-5 My Dream World By Rashma Mehta	978-1-910499-69-6 Consciousness By Mustak Mustafa	978-1-910499-40-5 World's First University By Giasuddin Ahmed
978-1-910499-50-4 Book of Lived v5 By Penny Authors	978-1-910499-53-5 Angel Eyez By Rashma Mehta	978-1-910499-73-3 Book of Lived v7 By Penny Authors	978-1-910499-56-6 The Warrior Queen By Giasuddin Ahmed

ISBN/Titles /Image/Author	ISBN/Titles /Image/Author	ISBN/Titles /Image/Author	ISBN/Titles /Image/Author
978-1-910499-58-0 Tower Hamlets, Random, One Mayar Akash	978-1-910499-60-3 Tower Hamlets, Random, Two By Mayar Akash	978-1-910499-05-4 Tide of Change By Mayar Akash	978-1-910499-51-1 Brick & Mortar By Mayar Akash
978-1-910499-61-0 Grenfell Tower By Mayar Akash	978-1-910499-63-4 Power Houses By Mayar Akash	978-1-910499-71-9 Altab Ali Murder By Mayar Akash	978-1-910499-31-3 Pathfinders By Mayar Akash
978-1-910499-62-7 Community Service 1992-1993 By Mayar Akash	978-1-910499-64-1 Bancroft Estate By Mayar Akash	978-1-910499-11-5 Re-Awakening By Mayar Akash	978-1-910499-13-9 Chronicle of Sylhetis of UK By Mayar Akash
978-1-910499-59-7 Brick Lane, Spitalfields By Mayar Akash	978-1-910499-72-6 25th Anniversary of Bangladesh By Mayar Akash	978-1-910499-12-2 Young Voice Mayar Akash	978-1-910499-42-9 Bangladeshi Fishes By Mayar Akash
978-1-910499-65-8 PYO Polish Exchange 1992 By Mayar Akash	978-1-910499-30-6 TH Bangladeshi Politicians By Mayar Akash	978-1-910499-10-8 Vigil Subotaged By Mayar Akash	978-1-910499-67-2 F. Ahmed and History By Mukid Choudhury

ISBN/Titles /Image/Author	ISBN/Titles /Image/Author	ISBN/Titles /Image/Author	ISBN/Titles /Image/Author
978-1-910499-43-6 My Life Book 1 By Mayar Akash	978-1-910499-44-3 My Life Book 2 By Mayar Akash	978-1-910499-45-0 My Life Book 3 By Mayar Akash	978-1-910499-46-7 My Life Book 4 By Mayar Akash
978-1-910499-47-4 My Life Book 5 By Mayar Akash	978-1-910499-75-7 Bangladeshis in Manchester - Oral History, Part 1 By M.A. Mustak	978-1-910499-74-0 Peter Fox Artist (LE) A Re-enchantment of Contemporary Art By Peter Fox	978-1-910499-78-8 On The Seventh Day By Cosette Ratliff
978-1-910499-79-5 Altab Ali Life & Family By Mayar Akash	978-1-910499-77-1 Smiley & the Acorn Treasure on the Isles of Scilly By Roger Underwood	978-1-910499-80-1 India – stories from the Banyan Tree Paul Wadsworth	978-1-910499-84-9 V8 Book of lived Penny Authors
978-1-910499-87-0 Behind the tears Rashma Mehta	978-1-910499-85-6 RhythmScripts My Feet is just mine Libby Pentreath	978-1-910499-89-4 Podgy and the Delightful Company John Dillon	978-1-910499-90-0 Calm and the Storm Alison Norton

www.mapublisher.org.uk